All
Rivers
Run
to the
Sea

Books by Joyce Hifler

ALL RIVERS RUN TO THE SEA

TO EVERY THING A SEASON

THINK ON THESE THINGS

DOUBLEDAY & COMPANY, INC.   GARDEN CITY, NEW YORK

1971

All Rivers Run to the Sea

Joyce Hifler

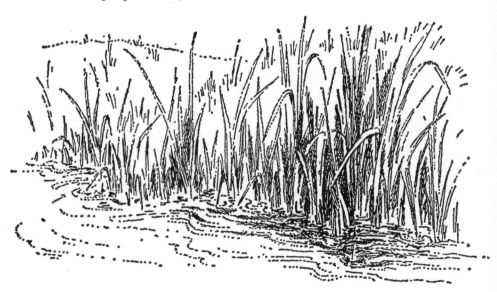

Excerpt from "Sea Fever" taken from the book POEMS by John
Masefield. Copyright 1912 by The Macmillan Company, renewed
1940 by John Masefield. Reprinted by permission of The Macmillan
Company and The Society of Authors.

Dedicated to my daughter, Jane,
and to
Papa, Charles Arch Sequichie, Jr.

CONTENTS

There is a dream I have dreamed so many times. It is a dream of rivers, all kinds of rivers, gentle, shallow, deep, turbulent, flooding, rocky, smooth, but *always flowing*. I have watched them from great heights, from very near, in fear and in quiet peace. But from these dreams I have learned that truly all rivers do run to the sea. These were the turbulent, the peaceful, the depths and shallow places of my life. And they were all building within me a central point to which all my rivers flow and from which all life abounds.

The place from where the rivers come, there they go again. It is life on a cycle, the endless, limitless infinity, born and reborn, alive to the fullest!

*All
Rivers
Run
to the
Sea*

1

*All rivers
run to the sea;
yet the sea is not full . . .*

*The eye is the first circle; the
horizon which it forms is the second;
and throughout nature this primary
picture is repeated without end. It
is the highest emblem in the cipher
of the world.*

Ralph Waldo Emerson

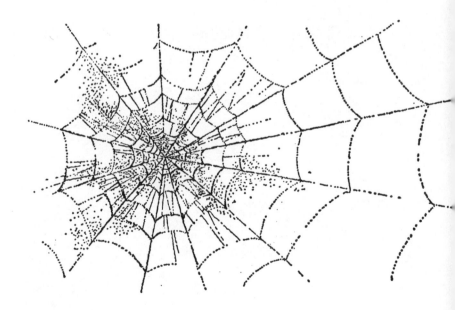

Rivers, like people, carry responsibility according to their inner size. It is not always possible to tell by looking at a river how deep it is. There are hints of shallow places, but there are also hidden depths. Said Henry van Dyke, "The life of a river, like that of a human being, consists in the union of soul and body, the water and the banks. They belong together. They act and react upon each other."

The river is the lifestream of the land. It takes its moisture from the air, flows to the sea and returns to the air. The cycle is endless, the similarity to man is unique. Within him is a lifestream that circulates again and again to renew his life.

There is a constant flow of life, a never-ending cycle that has no beginning and no ending. "All rivers run to the sea; and yet the sea is not full . . ." Ecclesiastes tells us. Are we not so? We eat and drink our fill, and yet we eat and drink again. We perform our daily duties, and they are yet to be done again. We think through a problem, and then we either think through the same one again or take a new one.

Each part of life is but a little cycle or a large cycle according to its importance. We learn and learn, and yet we cannot know it all. We love and love, and yet we cannot love enough. But we were granted something extra. We were given the ability to think. As life follows cycle after cycle, we are not programed to instinct nor do we follow the route of least resistance like the river, but with each spiraling cycle we can come up higher.

The woods in early morning has many wonders, but few more fascinating than the spider's web. I paused on the woodland path to watch her spin her circular net between two small trees. It was so exquisitely formed, like a remnant of gossamer, glittering with thousands of dewdrops. The threads were so delicately woven they reminded me of the lace my mother used to tat, and yet to this creature her work was not art but her home, her trap for food, her total universe. As I lightly touched one of the threads the whole web vibrated with the subtle workings of the spider as she tried to catch me in her web. And yet so unaware of me, she, being the first aeronaut, first builder, first spinner and weaver, had not progressed beyond her original programing. She could spin a splendid strand of silk, stronger in proportion to size and weight than the finest steel compounded to build the radial lines for the spokes to her wheel. She can anchor and mend and use prudent methods and care in the building of her web, but it will always be the same web, built again and again— her whole world.

I went on down the path, taking care not to spoil her morning's work. Maybe someone in passing my own cycle of the day will see and understand my motives and will continue on, allowing me to spin in privacy. Unlike the spider, I must spin better than I did yesterday. My work must be upward and forward, making daily improvements, for there are many rooms to my spinning.

Man's life is a river. And itself moves in a stream.

The most marvelous thing about all the faiths, creeds, denominations and mystic beliefs is the one purpose for which they exist. Man needs to worship. He may cut a tree, build a fire, cook his food, but with what he has left he will build something to worship or something to worship in. Whatever he chooses to do, he can be sure he will be criticized by others doing the same thing in a different way.

Every man is a river that flows within every group of worshipers to the great sea of believers. Each group of believers is a river running to the Great Source from which it came. There is a golden thread of sameness that runs through every person, the need to believe in something great and marvelous, all-wise and—above all else —all-loving. It is sad that so few find that last quality to be the essence of their belief, or indeed even within themselves. To so many, loving is simply a personal feeling that can be extended to everyone only by the sainted and the unusual. But as limiting as such a belief might be, every so often a bit of illumination breaks through and man feels a personal and universal love so vast and so deep that it cannot be measured by finite standards. It is a love of infinite pity and infinite pardon. This love is everywhere! It is impossible to conceive of a place where it is not. It not only envelopes the whole world, the whole universe, but any and all worlds beyond. This love, in itself and of itself, is God. It can only be made more beautiful by living it. And to live it means to allow only love and kindness to flow through our personal affairs so as to touch everything and everyone with truth. And truth is not a creed, but a light that illumines all creeds.

God has walked with me all day today. He keeps repeating, "Get up! Get up and do!"

And then there follows, "Rest." "Think, look up, remember, forget, heal, hope, grow young, be peaceful, patience!" AND THEN, "KNOW!"

2

*The tide
goes out,
another comes in . . .*

The stars come nightly to the sky,
The tidal wave unto the sea;
Nor time nor space, nor deep nor high,
Can keep my own away from me.

John Burroughs

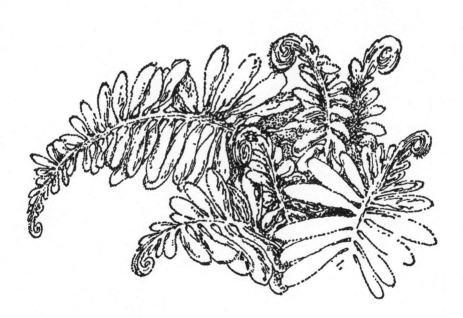

Life has rhythm. Even the tides at sea recede at regular intervals. If it were not so the sea would cover the land and break the order and discipline of nature.

There can be rhythm in our own lives. We seem always off to one extreme or other, fearing relaxation will cause us to lose the race. But there are always two sides to living. It makes life new. It helps us wisely wait our turn. If we do not, we are out of order, and if we are out of order, we lose the race anyway.

How like going through a collection of old purses is a nostalgic trip back the way we came. There is such a rare collection of things we consciously forget.

. . . an envelope of pain pills that reminded of times when things were so painful that nothing gave relief— and yet somehow with time relief came because of the willingness to wait for a pill or a prayer to do its work.

. . . wadded up tissues that should have been thrown out with the waste-basket litter that will collect in life if we ever have a thought that "this doesn't count" and allow it to collect in some hidden corner.

. . . the lost keys to the house, which symbolize the frequently lost keys to the rooms of our consciousness.

It is so easy to forget what we have stored away to deal with and which rooms need to be aired to allow full use.

. . . a small school photo of a nephew that is dear again. It seemed lately as he matured we lost patience and forgot how well he began—and then we have confidence that as the twig is bent, so grows the tree.

. . . a nickel that doesn't really go far any more. But like the five senses each penny in it plays a part. When it is invested in the right experiences all five can produce much of great value, and it returns again and again to enhance this day as richly as it served the day it was first shuffled away in an old purse to await a time when life gets too curious to stay lost for long and makes a new beginning.

The circle is one of the oldest figures in mathematics. But it does not take a mathematician to see his own life and how the simplest bits of his living travel on a cycle. It is true that the straight line is the simplest line, but the circle is the simplest non-straight line. We cannot always push straight to whatever it is we want of life. It is so often necessary to go out around our actual goal before we can curve back and touch the high point we have been trying to reach.

How deep and mysterious are these laws of life that direct us away from our objectives, sometimes in order to bring us back to them with a certainty of success.

There is a little stone walk down to the water, and a wooden bridge that crosses over—in fact, there is more bridge than water—gives a full view of the woods on both sides of the little stream. As I stood in the middle of the bridge looking upstream and watching the water work the easiest way down through the sand stones and over tree roots to ripple out of sight under the bridge, I laughed as I listened to my philosopher-artist friend who had come down to do an oil of the old bridge. "Why, you couldn't let a dozen cats trot across that bridge at one time, or they would set up a vibration that would shake it down." Really, it is quite a sturdy bridge, sturdy enough to pass over in a horse cart.

I make this first little trek very early in the morning, starting from the back of the house down the walk, across the bridge, up the long flight of stone steps to woods and then upstream along a private path known only to me, I pretend. It is like the path I used to follow as a child, hidden away beneath fern fronds and woods plants so abundant and so full of new growth they snap like celery hearts, and it is such a shame to break any of them. In spring, the plum blossoms scent the whole woods and the redbuds blend pink and red with the dogwood. In summer, there are bunches of goldenrod and fragrant violets in sun and shadow, and in fall, clusters of red berries hang heavily among the last green leaves. Then all wild colors of chrysanthemums float idly down to cover places on the beaten path.

Winter affords breath-taking views of things I cannot see for the heavy foliage during the rest of the year. Only now can I detect the animals of the woods and see the birds. I love to carry a pocket of grain to scatter along the path. And now they have begun to treat me as a friend and not a foe. The little waterfall sings a higher tune in winter and the neighbor's cowbell rings clearly across the woods. It is at this point that I cross back over the stream, stepping on the rocks, doing it slowly to see the water rile from beneath and at the same time feel the sun warm on my back and head.

Henry David Thoreau talked of this when he talked of Walden Pond. "Walden is blue at one time and green at another," he said, "even from the same point of view.

Lying between the earth and the heavens, it partakes of the color of both."

Viewed from early morning, this beauty is all pink and gold. At noon it is the color of yellow buttercups, and in the late afternoon is like an emerald set in platinum only to be edged out by topaz. At night it is pale-blue chiffon, glowing pearl and silver with moonlight.

On my way back I stopped to see how the oil painting was progressing. He was just putting away his color box, but he took time for the wisdom I expected. "One thing about it," he said as he spat over the side of the bridge, "you can't spit in the same water twice. No point in runnin' after it. It's gone now—water under the bridge."

With that I felt an excitement that always comes at this time. Coming home has ever been a special joy of mine no matter how short the trip. Besides the warmth of fireside, savory kitchen aromas, music, good books and happiness—something else awaits—love. Some bits of life we don't have to run after—they come to meet us.

Shakespeare writes, in *Julius Caesar*, "There is a tide in the affairs of men which taken at the floods leads on to fortune; omitted, all the voyage of their life is bound in shallows and in miseries."

To be bound in shallows is to be miserable. And not a few of us have already known the feeling of being caught on dry land like some great whale unable to move without the tide to buoy us up and fearing there would not soon be another tide strong enough or high enough to float us out again. It is a desperate feeling to be on high ground and see other ships passing by on their way to interesting ports with cargoes of valuable goods.

It is said that time or tide wait for no man. The tide must go out when it is programed to go. There is no waiting while a ship finishes its loading, no holding back while the sea life gets safely back into deeper water. The only way to catch the tide is to be *ready* when it rolls out again.

Man keeps waiting to do one more thing before he takes the tide out to his own fortune. His selfish motives tell him not to move from his place on the beach because someone else will get it. And after all, why give up a sure thing like a square foot of drifting sand for what only appears to be a whole ocean full out there? To sail away would mean leaving behind these few things that someone might get credit for having accomplished—someone besides self. Or even worse is to stay for spite—to spite whom?

Those who must fear missing the most important flood tide of their lives are not those who have been alert, working, thinking and planning, but those who long ago washed up and have not moved since. They have no foundation, no true faith—although they do have some hope—no activity to keep supple their minds and spirits, no thought of anything for the real good of mankind, but only dreams of the fulfillment of their own self-glorification.

Live weight is always easier to buoy up and carry than dead weight. Life means not only dreams, but plans to make those dreams come true, and activity to make those plans work, and work to make those actions lead to fortunes! Why be bound in shallows when the flood tide may be any day?

Harriet Beecher Stowe once wrote, "When you get in a tight place and everything goes against you, till it seems as though you could not hold on a minute longer, never give up then, for that is just the place and time that the tide will turn."

There are two roads we can follow when we reach such places in life. One is up and the other is down. If we quit, we do not have to worry about choosing, we just naturally gravitate downward. If we choose to keep trying to make things work, we need to learn how to pause and listen while we work. It is frequently during the periods of silence and rest that the tide suddenly turns.

3

*The sun
also rises,
and the sun goes down* . . .

There are from time to time mornings, both in summer and in winter, when especially the world seems to begin anew . . . mornings of creation, I call them. In the midst of these marks of creative energy recently active, while the sun is rising with more than usual splendor, I look back . . . for the era of this creation, not into the night, but to a dawn for which no man ever rose early enough. A morning carries us back beyond the Mosaic creation, where crystallizations are fresh and unmelted. It is the poet's hour. Mornings when men are new-born, men who have the seeds of life in them.

Henry David Thoreau

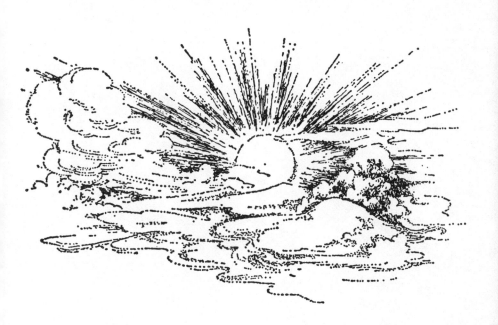

There are times when my spirit escapes the world completely and soars above the earth's atmosphere to where unlimited freedom exists. . . . It soars where the morning sun ripens from pink to gold . . . to where the gull escapes the green tinge of the sea below.

My spirit soars to lunar heights where Job's stars sang together at dawn . . . but then, sometimes it becomes dull, covered over with the smoke and dust of idleness . . . and weighted down with weariness and apathy and ugliness . . . but worse than any of these—hopelessness.

Then something happens to change its direction . . . not some outside influence . . . but the spirit within was ready to soar again . . . ready on its own, and it merely opened up and received nourishment or illumination to soar again . . . this time even higher and all I remember is that each time it lifts up . . . it remains on a higher level . . .

I need only to know that no matter if it glides downward again . . . I know now that it can shake off the negative attitudes and fly again to even greater heights and more freedom than ever before.

Reflection is not always accurate. When a pebble is dropped in still water, the ripples do not allow the sun to reflect in its own round image, but distort the edges like an egg yolk broken across the waves. Reflections of life are apt to be that way. We need to take into account the ripples of memory.

There is a lot of water under the bridge between sunrise and sunset. A day full of change, a day's worth of effort, endurance, patience, some gains, some wisdom, but always an education when we are looking for an education. There is a little bit of learning in every person, in every situation when we can stop thinking about it in connection with ourselves and study it objectively.

People are like trees full of leaves—they may look alike, but a little closer observation will show that they are uniquely different, every shape and size and varying greatly in color.

Association, people, life; twenty-four hours, eight hours, fifteen seconds can make all the difference in living.

Leaves, all colors of chrysanthemums, gild the autumn hills and daub red all along the landscape. So much that was green and lush now lies dormant, resting for another birth, another burst of life. And here in air clear and brisk, yet warm in the sunlight, the brown path beneath my feet leads me farther up the hill.

At the highest point, I turn and look across the valleys and view the scene below. Rustic brown rooftops seem to be only smooth spots partially hidden by the thick growth of trees and splashes of color. Now the red barns are more easily hidden than many things much smaller. Now the world is their color.

If I can feel such exhilaration standing here viewing the beauty from this small spot, think what the Almighty must feel to see the magnificence of the whole universe. My heart also says, "It is good." And to make sure it knows my feelings, I cup my hands to my mouth and call out,

"Hel-lo, Wor-ld!"

And I hear it pass the hollows and hills and reverberate until it bounces back to me, "Hel-lo, Wor-ld . . ." I sent it out and it made its cycle and came back several times. It is the Law of the Echo that what we send out we get back so many times. Around and around it spins past hollow and place after place we do not even know about to return to this spot where I stand. I sent it out and I got it back.

My voice, my thought, my action go out into the world, and as small as they may seem, they touch places, places I do not dream of, and return to me multiplied in whatever form I sent them out—good or bad—I am also under the Law of the Echo.

Two persons, equally intelligent, equally cared for and about, find themselves at close of day. One has only to fret aloud that the day had been unfulfilling, unreasonable and a total loss. The other says nothing, but the expression of gratitude for the hours past rests comfortably in her face and in the very atmosphere.

To whom does life turn with blessings—the one who complains of the dragging hours, or the one who sees the sun rise with great opportunity to be happy and sees it set with even greater thanksgiving?

Who am I? The blessed one or the one from whom life turns away?

The capacity of some to accept the good of life when it comes to them seems awfully meager at times. There is a tendency to be forever testing even the ordinary events to see if they are real or worthwhile.

There are things, feelings, thoughts that have to be accepted on face value, at least for the moment. Swallowing everything hook, line and sinker is not necessary, but a constant pecking away at even the strongest can eventually destroy anything important.

Sometimes our desire to test everyone and everything is not because of the lack of confidence in them, but the lack of security within ourselves.

4

The wind
blows to the south
and turns to the north . . .

Who has seen the wind?
Neither you nor I:
But when the trees bow down their heads,
The wind is passing by.

Christina Georgina Rossetti

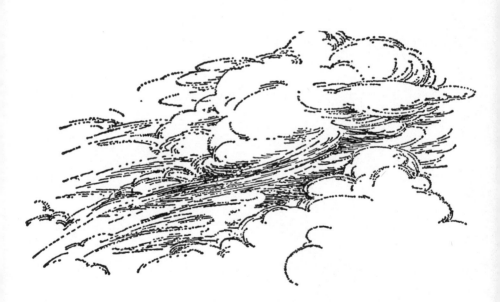

We can almost resent the wind blowing because it can be so downright unpleasant. But the wind is like circumstance; it serves a purpose to make the seasons go forward. It is necessary to blow away winter and to bring in the moisture to feed the green fields.

Sometimes we resent the changes in our lives. They seem so unnecessary. We treat them as intruders, but like the seasons, before we can experience anything worthy and produce anything worth reaping we must move out of winter and into the spring.

Changes, like the wind, must be endured for a time. But if we are patient, we are sure to understand and perhaps like the results.

The picnic table was laden with hot dogs, relishes, mustard, rolls, ice cream and tea. The children puttered around the charcoal grill and laughingly got in my way, as they had all afternoon, while we cleaned the back porch. The summer heat had us all feeling a little soiled and overcooked, but our spirits were high because we had worked together successfully. The clouds overhead were gathering and I predicted rain before the evening was over.

In a matter of minutes the wind stirred the shrubs and the elm trees started to toss. Little Janie shuddered and said she was cold. Annette, who believes what she reads, but a little fearfully, said, "Peace be still!" I told them, "The wind is changing."

After a few minutes of holding down the tablecloth, watching the grill and grabbing our napkins, my daughter said quietly, "That's life." I asked what she meant and she said, "One person is uncomfortable because of a change, one is afraid but faithful and another simply says there is a change and goes about preparing for it."

The eye is not satisfied to see; nor the ear to hear . . .

The sea awoke at midnight from its sleep
And round the pebbly beaches far and wide
I heard the first wave of the rising tide
Rush onward with uninterrupted sweep

A voice out of the silence of the deep,
A sound mysteriously multiplied
As of a cataract from the mountain's side,
Or roar of winds upon a wooded steep.

So comes to us at times, from the unknown
And inaccessible solitudes of being,

The rushing of the sea-tides of the soul;
And inspirations, that we deem our own,
Are some divine foreshadowing and foreseeing
Of things beyond our reason or control.

Henry Wadsworth Longfellow

When things get too much for us we tend to think we are no longer able to do anything about it and give up without further effort. In James it is written, "Behold also the ships, which though they be great, and are driven of fierce winds, yet are they turned about with a very small helm . . ."

We are also very small and seemingly ineffective at times. But when we feel driven by fierce winds, we can remember that faith, fortitude and a steadfast determination has changed many a defeat to a success.

An old French proverb runs, "Some of your griefs you have cured, and the sharpest you still have survived; but what torments of pain you endured, from evils that never arrived."

For most of us the experiences that tax our strength

are small in comparison to those we imagine. We insist on crossing bridges that are not there. We are determined to experience every difficulty twice, once when we worry and once when it happens. And most of the time it never happens, so we have wasted good time worrying once.

We are not always satisfied to see or hear what is true. We are more apt to let our imaginations take wild skirmishes into areas where we have no business.

A whirlwind has a fierce personality. It can pick up missiles so small it is impossible to see them, but how they sting bare feet and legs.

As children, we thought it was fun to run into the center of a whirlwind and settle it. However uncomfortable it was, it gave us a sense of superiority to be able to stop the force of the circular air current simply by standing still.

With maturity I discovered the same rule applied to everyday whirlwinds. When I refuse to go around and around with them, they lose their force. But, if I throw trash into the wind by thought or word or action, I get trash back on the next spin—and how it stings!

❃

While the desert fainted for moisture the Nile was carrying millions of tons of water to the sea, and a tiny seed lay dormant but filled with intelligence on the now dried slime where once the river had overflowed.

Famine had taken many of those who threw the seeds under a pitiless, burning sun rolling away into the distance. They had been half-blinded and half-frightened by this immense wasteland. Generations had believed it was an act of God; something that passes the power of man to alter. But when they saw the mud cover their land they took fresh heart and tried once again to grow food. But it takes only a tiny seed in the mind of man to look at a desert and say, "This can be altered . . ."

As it is intended, the seed in the mind of man and the seed lying dormant in nature join forces and through the diversion of water resources make the desert bloom and provide food for man. Through the co-operation of man and nature life is preserved—because of the marvel that man says again and again, "This can be altered . . ."

5

The rivers come,
and go there again . . .

It is with rivers as it is with people;
the greatest are not always the most agreeable
nor the easiest to live with . . .

Henry van Dyke

A river that is not deep enough to hold all the water that flows into it during a rainy season is in danger of flooding, and when it overflows everything near it can be damaged or destroyed. For this reason, people living in such areas give the river a wide berth, refusing to build anything of value where it can be touched.

Shallow people are not dependable either. Never having been dredged out by time or circumstance, they do not control, nor are they able to contain a sudden change. They lash out at anything in their way. It is for this reason that others build walls for their own protection.

Anyone knowing how important the power of water is to industry and farms and to the life of the land, knows that the river must live. It is the lifestream, the activity necessary to support everything small and great.

Man also has a lifestream over and above his physical being. It is that which supports him in his efforts to be better, to ignore pessimism and to know that nothing is too good to be true, nothing is too wonderful to happen. It is something within that demands life, and we must keep it clean and free-flowing, singing and full of lively imagination. It is the stream of life—and faith.

In spring, the river is young and full and rushing in all its youth. It carries with it the first green leaves pulled from low-hanging branches. The clear, free-flowing water sings clean and fresh. It has not yet had time to pick up debris. Soon rains will cause it to overflow its banks, and when it gets too full it gets a little wild and tends to be destructive.

But summer will tone it down. It can hardly be wild when it finds itself sluggish with too much to carry with it. Only midstream finds any clear water, and even there it is murky from picking up everything along the way. It is warm and slow, giving way to pools and eddies where snags and hazards are not visible to the navigator's eye.

Autumn finds the river cooler, clearer and colorful with autumn leaves all shades of brilliant yellow, reds and golds. Trees, like tall rustling taffetas, border its banks and drop leaves like confetti on the flowing water. Geese, honking their way south, find refuge on the smooth surface, and fish flip their tails to catch low flying insects that hover just above the water.

In winter, the river is deeper, still-running and a little murky from house-cleaning after autumn. It is no longer framed in color, but has on its winter look like a sophisticated lady. Sycamores stand white along the banks, and cardinal wings flash red through the dark woods. Mink and raccoon come down to drink, and deer, lithe and elusive, leap in and out of sight.

Every river has its cycle of seasons. Each season has its specialty on the river—beautiful, natural and orderly. Like the seasons of man it is alive with hidden activity, preparing continually for the next splendid season—all on its fascinating rush to the sea.

Rivers have personalities just like people. Rivers are like people in many ways—long, thin, wide, deep, shallow, murky, crystal clear, full of debris, rapid and babbling!

It is said that a river has no active power until it is harnessed. Does man have power when he is pent up? Is he not like the river when the power is not used constructively? The river overflows and drowns, destroys and becomes a menace. Water dammed is kept at a sensible level. It is released at a rate that keeps it flowing free and active, and it is maintained at a level beneficial to its purpose. Like man, if there is no discipline, it will meander around the countryside doing nothing worthwhile. But when there is work to be done, it can replenish the land and transport power and give life.

Man's words are like the river. They must be withheld and used with wisdom to be productive. If he talks all the time, he is scattering his forces and saying nothing really important. It takes away any build-up of power he may have been working for, and instead of success he may have it delayed or even defeated. Words have the worth of water, used wisely they produce life. In a runaway condition they distort and destroy.

6

The crooked
is not straight,
the wanting is not numbered . . .

Drop a stone into the water—
In a moment it is gone.
But there are a hundred ripples
Circling on and on and on.
Say an unkind word this moment—
In a moment it is gone.
But there are a hundred ripples
Circling on and on and on.
Say a word of cheer and splendor—
In a moment it is gone.
But there are a hundred ripples
Circling on and on and on.

Anonymous

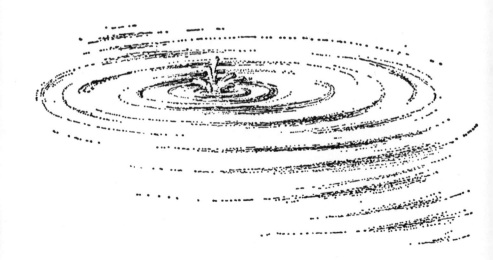

I am a river that in the beginning flowed young and was easily recognized for my steep banks. Because I was narrow and swift I took up all the space I could find in the valley of life to cut twists and turns in an effort to find an easy way to the sea.

With some maturity, my banks are not so steep. I am more gentle, for there is no longer a need to occupy all the valley. Now I am able to accomplish more by thoughtfully cutting through some of the turns and bends to make straighter my journey to the sea.

In my journey I have started new cycles by carrying along some of the substance to deposit here and there to uplift the bed over which I flow.

I cannot straighten everything that I have made crooked, but I can make use of the experience, and leave straighter the way for the tributaries that will flow into my mainstream.

The meaning, or value, of all experiences will come out in the wash. When it seems we are put through a little more hell than we think we are capable of bearing, it is usually because we feel we are experiencing something without a reason. It seems that if we could understand why we are going through this experience, it would somehow justify the pain.

There are moments that etch character in the face and

do either of two things to the heart—strengthen and make it more loving, or give it over to bitterness. To forgive leaves the door open for something better to come in. Bitterness closes the door with all the trouble on the inside.

Who knows why? Is it something beyond our comprehension? Is there a tempering that prepares us for something, someone or some purpose that will require us to be greater than we are presently able to be?

All rivers run to the sea. Everything has a meaning. All meanings have a purpose. If we are patient, if we are forgiving that we must have this experience—as was Job—without explanation or encouragement, then our ultimate lives can be excellent.

When we figure that the miles between home and work over a period of time equals about ten times around the world, it makes us wonder how many other circles we have been making without realizing it. Some are not so important as going to work.

The tempestuous, tossing sea, which seems in such chaos when we look at it, has regular, never-ceasing currents running through it. These are rivers that stay on course without the benefit of beds or banks to hold them.

There are many currents that affect the climate of the world, but the greatest and most important is the Gulf Stream. This great circle of water has within its center quiet water that collects seaweed in such a large area that early sea travelers were slowed or trapped. Columbus overcame it by his persistent, "Sail on!"

Man and nature have so much in common. There is a need for both to have inner discipline in order to maintain a certain course. And yet, there is a difference because the stream is controlled by the order of the universe—and man stays on course by choice.

"Alone?" he asked. "No, I'm never alone. I have my friends always with me . . . my trees . . . my

flowers . . . the honey bees . . . my vegetable garden."
And he smiled merrily while he fingered his white
beard around ruddy cheeks.

"One is never alone with things he loves and things
that love him." His eyes twinkled good-naturedly and
his hand kept wandering down to stroke the satiny
head of a dog with questionable heritage.

"And who could be alone with Emerson and Thoreau
and the memories of all the people I have known in a
lifetime and all those, like you, whom I will know."

"Yes, I go down to the sea now and again." He answered a question. "Like John Masefield, 'I must go
down to the seas again, to the lonely sea and the sky, and
all I ask is a tall ship and a star to steer her by . . .'

"I think perhaps our love for things sometimes is our
awe of them . . . as long as they fascinate and intrigue
us we stand in complete mystery with our emotions
sometimes bordering on fear . . . like for the sea, for
instance."

He paused to contemplate the rapid-fire questions of
his peers, sometimes letting one pass in favor of a more
intelligent one.

"You say you know the world is turning, but you
can't see it," and he laughed aloud for the humor and
depth of the thought. "Of course, the world is turn-

ing . . . your world is turning every minute . . . don't be impatient . . . you need that precious time to get to know who you are . . . to pace yourself to the wisdom of nature . . . to tune yourself to the sweetness of the Almighty, who so carefully created you . . . believe in that, believe in yourself . . . every day envision yourself as a beautiful fulfilled person, serving and being served . . ."

And as though he had revealed too much at a time, he spent moments going within as though none of us were there. And somehow we respected that regeneration of thought and remained silent until he looked up and smiled very quickly.

"No, I do not think the crooked things of the world can be *made* straight . . . I do think we are given enough space and time to straighten ourselves. Thoreau once said, 'How vain to try to teach youth, or anybody, truths! They can only learn them after their own fashion, and when they get ready . . .' But, one can never tell when he will encounter the very youth who is ready . . . and that is worth all the effort of teaching those who are merely recording fact, but are not turned on in the heart . . ."

The dog, the obedient friend, suddenly got to its feet beside him, and as though it reminded him that he had other things to do, he spread his gnarled hands toward us as if in silent blessing, and added joyfully,

"Be happy . . . there's so little need to ever be otherwise . . . and there is so much beauty to inhale and enjoy."

He beamed on each of us and continued, "In the words of Hypatia, 'It is but a little time . . . a few days longer in this prison house of our degradation, and each thing shall return to its own fountain; the blood-drop to the abysmal heart, and the water to the river, and the river to the shining sea; and the dewdrop which fell from heaven shall rise to heaven again, shaking off the dust grains which weighted it down, thawed from the earth frost which chained it here to herb and sward, up-ward and upward ever through stars and suns, through gods, and through the parents of the gods purer and purer through successive lives, until it enters The Noth-ing, which is the All, and finds its home at last.'

"My love," he said.

There is a very high quiet, far beyond the speed of sound, that invites each of us to find peace within our-selves. How diligently we search for it elsewhere, wishing for some sort of magic carpet to whisk us away to a peaceful place. And we often discover how short-lived is that magic.

Peace is not a forced habit, it is a relaxed practice. It is the knowledge beyond the thought that in this quiet moment I cannot turn the world around and yet in releasing the burden allow it to begin adjustments.

To rise above our emotions, to control and release the tension, will allow peace to flow to us. Sometimes when we cannot forcefully straighten out our lives we can take our hands off and allow it to improve naturally.

7

That
which has been
shall be . . .

*If I listen, I hear the peep of frogs
which is older than the slime of Egypt, and
the distant drumming of a partridge on a log,
as if it were the pulsebeat of the summer air . . .
The newest is but the oldest made visible to
our senses.*

Henry David Thoreau

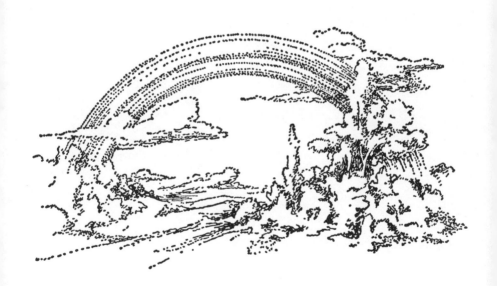

The rainbow's half circle of color arching the sky is the essence of perfect blending . . . color upon color, the master pallet . . . repeated and repeated like the old, old promise that all is well.

We can have a rainbow within ourselves . . . the colors rich beyond belief and called such beautiful names . . . simplicity, concern, gentleness, joy!

When we can arch upward with the clean sweep of the rainbow . . . with the promise within ourselves that all is well . . . that love and beauty of life is the ultimate . . . then all the lavish color of the rainbow will shine through us.

That which has been done shall be done . . .

Again I saw, again I heard
the rolling river, the morning bird;
Beauty through my senses stole;
I yielded myself to the perfect whole.

Ralph Waldo Emerson

Through the ages autumn has returned again and again to uplift us with its cool, crisp breezes, to charm us with its ability to maintain a little of summer with a bit of winter. Nature may vary a little in its timing, but the amount is so minute we seldom recognize the difference.

Only man can look at his daily pace that seems unchangeable and say, "Maybe . . ." and proceed to change. It doesn't matter what the season for he does not have to follow a set pattern but is free to think, plan and organize.

If only now man can learn to think, plan, organize and, most important, control, he can be a winner. He is too often prone to fall under the power of his own organization. In this respect, nature still is the wiser.

"Nothing to do? My goodness, everyone has something to do! I can give you dozens of things you can do and have fun doing.

"Usually when people feel they have nothing to do

it is because they are tired of doing the same old things . . . and there is always a need to rest from routine things. Sometimes we just get tired of being who we are, and we need a rest from that, too.

"Let me tell you how to be whatever you want to be. Go outside and lie down on your back on the grass, and stare straight up into the open sky and allow your eyes to keep going and going . . . see how limitless it is? There is nothing to stop you from seeing as far as you want to see . . . nothing between you and all the heavens. Now imagine who you would like to be . . . all grown up . . . an elf, perhaps . . . finding a pot of gold at the end of the rainbow . . . seeing a star up close . . . or a fairy princess with wardrobes and wardrobes of gossamer gowns and diamond tiaras . . .

"Oh, yes, you can be a fairy princess! Have I ever told you the story of the caterpillar? I haven't? My goodness, how could I have missed doing that? It is such a beautiful story . . . one that begins long before the caterpillar comes into being. There is this beautiful butterfly with golden wings that spread this wide . . . and are decorated with white and brown polka dots and other beautiful designs too unusual to remember right now. She lays her eggs and places food there for the babies to eat when they are born and then she goes far away. When the babies are born they find the food and eat until they are stronger and able to begin their own way of life.

"Soon they are large caterpillars storing enough food to live on, and they can build themselves a silken home to live in. They usually build it high above the ground —for safety—and they weave the web and pull the very fine fibers so to make a strong cocoon . . . and then they close themselves inside. Inside their new home they work magic of their own and change their appearance from that of a worm into something completely different. At the right moment they emerge from the cocoon by pushing themselves out the top, and then they sit for a while and let their wings dry.

"When they have dried they can open their wings and here once again is a beautiful, brightly colored butterfly. And she will begin a new cycle of laying eggs, feeding and so on.

"Why? Perhaps there is no set reason for anything existing. Maybe it is simply for us to see such exquisite beauty for however brief the time . . . but this we know . . . it is all necessary, because if it were not, the butterfly would never have been created. It is all a part of the fabric of life."

�֎

"Look there along the timber line . . . look close or you'll never see them. Once they get wind of you they're gone, or else they stand so still you have to focus your eyes to be able to spot them.

"Right about sundown they come out to graze. Sometime you can see ten or fifteen of them feeding along with the cattle . . . they know this is not hunting season, and they are just as curious about you as you are about them. Do you see any?

"There! There's one standin' near that big tree . . . and there's another doe and a buck with her! Did you ever seen anything so purty? Makes you sorry for all them deer you see in the zoos—no spirit—just like people when you haul 'em food they just kind of lay around waiting for the next time. But these whitetails are alive and free . . . even if they have to hunt for their food and be hunted sometimes—it's better this way.

"There, now move up a little closer . . . see the buck? He's a beauty! He's in the velvet now. Well . . . that means his horns are brand new . . . see the little humps . . . the little points on top of his head? They keep growing, but every year he starts a new one 'long

71

about now—in July—and then every year he adds another point to the rack, but by the time he gets around to February he's ready to shed the whole thing.

"No, it just doesn't fall off. He has to beat it off. Oh, it doesn't hurt him . . . probably like having a tooth pulled . . . but then I ain't never been a deer. Every once in a while when I'm walking through these woods of mine, I see a tree that is worn smooth on the bark . . . and I know it's some buck's whipping tree.

"And his color runs a cycle, too. Think the Creator hasn't given 'em everything? They start out fawn color, and by fall they're the exact color of blackjack leaves . . . all the colors in between, red to bronze, make 'em a part of the colors around.

"There they go! Flickerin' their white tails . . . but you ought to see 'em when they lift over a fence . . . like feathers they can rise in the air and sail over a five-wire fence without any strain at all . . . and then they can stand a short distance away and stare with faces as bashful as children and wise as sages.

"Come on, son, you're going to see a lot of beautiful things in your time . . . appreciate every bit of it . . . 'cause you're just now in the velvet."

If you ever start out to scuttle someone else's ship, quickly prepare for your own to sink.

It isn't that we have to fear the one we have set out to hurt, but there is a universal law that works in such a way that we get that which we give.

People so often wonder why they do not succeed, when their first thought is not so much to move ahead with a just attitude, but to put as many pitfalls as possible in the way of others so as to make them fall behind.

When we cause others to lose, we lose. Our opinion of what they deserve is not for our expression, unless we are strong enough to bear up under the opinions of others.

All of life travels on a cycle. We have the tendency to think "a beginning and an end," when it is "an end and a beginning."

When life closes one cycle it begins another. If we can take our attention away from everything that has passed, we can more easily see past the curve in the road ahead.

Life is never lived back there. Life is here. And as it is lived it moves on around the cycle requiring us to keep going—keep face forward—so as not to miss a single step. Only then do we have any understanding of the why of living. Only then, do we start a new and happier cycle.

8

*No memory
of former things,
nor of things to come . . .*

*Think often of the speed with which things
pass and disappear, both the things which are and
the things which are being produced. For matter is
like a river in a continual flow, and the activities
of things are constantly shifting, and the causes
work in infinite varieties; there is hardly anything
which stands still. And consider this which stands
near you, this boundless abyss of the past and the
future in which all things disappear. Why then
is he not a fool who is puffed up over such things or
plagued about them, making himself miserable? For
they vex him only for a time, and a very short
time.*

Marcus Aurelius

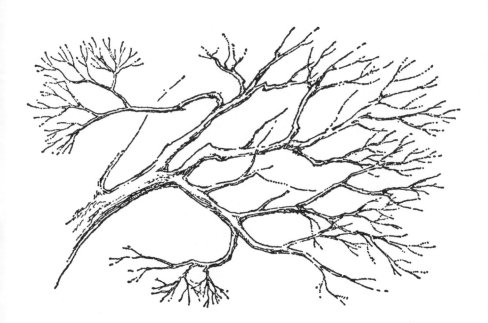

While we stand by a river and watch the gentle flow of water, it doesn't seem we are looking at power. The flow seems too slow and easy to have any strength. But this is a sort of "big little energy" that works in subtle ways to conceal its power.

Man walls up a river and outwardly the water conforms readily enough, but there is never a time that the river is not working against the dam. It is forever aided by the rain drops and by the smallest things of nature to make an imperceptible opening. If the smallest break-through is thought insignificant by man who believes only in his own skill, the river will come into its own, and the thunder of unleashed water will turn everything into kindling wood on its rush to the sea.

The pent-up emotions of man are forever working for expression. If there are forbidden feelings, not spent by expression, there is accumulated force, and when the emotional dam breaks it is more destructive than the steady current ever could have been.

When people continually see evil in everybody and in everything—when they steadily call attention to "this evil generation," which has been every generation's label from the beginning of time—there is a steady build-up of all that is wrong: guilt feelings, darkness, sickness, fear, anxiety, distrust, withdrawal. Man with all his research, takes pride in more and more of this and that by artificial means—and when the dam breaks it is not just a big little energy—it is plain ugly.

We were meant to be children of the light. We are meant to be spinners or workers in the sun. We are meant this day to be seers of good, weavers of dreams, steady, free-flowing currents of clean, gentle water, self-disciplined, but never dammed.

The evil? What about the evil? Like attracts like. To be a new creature, one lets go of evil, even to call it evil. One expounds not on the evil of evil, but on the good of good. Talk, think, pray, see and give thanks for what is wanted in life. Let the dead bury the dead. Come and follow what really counts—the cleanliness, the light, the vibrant good health, the freedom of being happy and joyful from the inside out and not from trying to create spiritual experiences by artificial means. Flow clean, flow steady—but flow!

Infinity, the circle of wholeness. The constant, revolving turn of events that are ever old, yet eternally new. Like the sun, the moon, the planets, the ground on which we stand is holy, for it is a part of the great ball of creativity revolving in time.

The circle as a symbol of completion in living is an invisible force that keeps us so alone in our evolution. We cannot see around the bend behind us, nor can our eyes take the curve ahead. No matter what mark we make that seems so stable, another person can come along and draw another circle around what we have accomplished.

Emerson wrote, "God delights to isolate us every day, and hide from us the past and future . . . 'You will not remember,' he seems to say, 'and you will not expect.'"

It is difficult to see the whole of anything when we are in the midst of it. We do not remember and we cannot run ahead, for if we could, the greatness of the present moment would be lost. We, like infinity, must run the whole cycle to completion.

Have we not heard it said, or said it ourselves, that we knew something was going to be a certain way? We had an inner sense of "knowing" that something was not only possible but probable.

What is this knowing except the ability of the mind to broadcast or receive? It has capabilities we do not dream exists. It projects, probes and investigates for information our conscious minds are not always willing to accept.

We consciously have no memory of former things, nor does it seem possible that we can know of things to come, and yet our wonderful sense of "knowing" insists we pay attention. Can we be honest enough to admit to ourselves that we subconsciously know more than we are willing to accept?

It is not what happened to us yesterday that makes the difference in our attitudes and behavior. It is the result of years past.

We have no idea how rooted our beliefs, thoughts and behavior patterns are in childhood. We try desperately to understand who we are by looking at our today's reflection. It is the childhood influence that holds the key.

Within every one of us is a path leading backward through a maze of forgotten incidents. Although forgotten consciously, they still lean heavily on us in all that we do to this very moment.

However we respond in any situation will be determined by how well we come to know who we were as children. That child is the one we must love, correct and understand before we can know who we are this day.

It is also true that I will never again be what I am at this moment. If it is not to my liking, I have only to wait another moment and it will have passed, too. Should it be a time of high experience, something worth remembering, then the memory will be only a new level from which to begin to go higher and do better.

Yesterday is only a memory and tomorrow, still a dream. "Right now" I can do something about.

It is this moment that makes or breaks me in the moment to come. Now is the important time.

9

Much wisdom;
much sadness . . .

*I am tired of fighting . . . my people
ask me for food, and I have none to give. It
is cold and we have no blankets, no wood. My
people are starving to death. Where is my little
daughter? I do not know . . .*

*Hear me, my Chiefs . . . I have fought; but from
where the sun now stands, I will fight no more
for as long as the grass shall grow and the
rivers flow. . . .*

*Chief Joseph
Nez Perce, Idaho
1877*

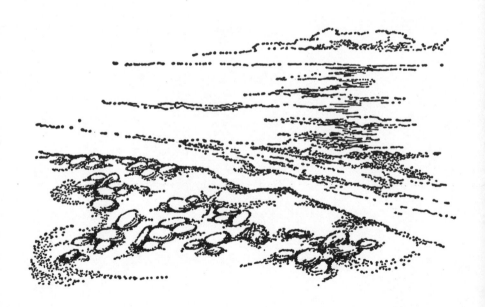

Alexander Pope wrote with satire, "Lo, the poor Indian! whose untutor'd mind sees God in clouds, or hears him in the wind."

The wonderful simplicity of the Indian's personal worship would cure many a troubled mind for those who have complicated their belief in something greater than themselves.

There is a sincerity in seeing God in the simplest things of nature. Where there are such beliefs there is a basic something in man's life on which he can depend. His love of all life is as universal as the clouds and the wind.

Gay spirits were the rule of the day. At least, for the most part. Our guide directed us along, showing us the many beauties of the place—trees and flowers and lakes, blue and clear. The mountains in the distance were blended blue to blue-gray with the haze hanging in the tall green pines.

We left our bus in the woods and went on foot along a stone pathway that descended down a slope and across a little bridge. The stones beneath our feet were wet from the summer shower and from moisture seeping out of the soft earth beneath the trees. The birds were singing and dogwood, like a great umbrella of white and pink petals, hung over our heads. Before us was a beautiful chapel standing on the edge of the lake.

It is very difficult to feel reverence for anything in a group of laughing, joking individuals. I had been closely associated with these people for days, and regardless of their good spirits, I felt worn from lack of rest and solitude. The quiet of the chapel was inviting and would have been a haven, but sightseers are often more interested in each other than in their surroundings.

I went apart from the others and sat down at the water's edge. For a few quiet moments I absorbed the rhythm and steady pulse of nature around me. The breeze picked up a maple leaf that had dried to cup shape and skidded it onto the surface of the water. It made a perfect little boat. A tiny frog thought so, too. It leaped from a clump of grass and landed on the edge of the leaf with one leg still kicking behind in an effort to get aboard while the leaf dipped and swooped. I thought to myself, *Frog, if you are smart you will quit kicking so hard and enjoy the dry raft you are floating on. One more kick and the lake will be in there with you.*

I am like the frog, I thought. I am in the world, but

I do not have to be of the world. It is like being in a ship afloat on the sea of humanity. I am in the ship, but I must not let the sea get in, too. I must be here, but I do not have to take everything that beats against my sides. If I let the whole sea of difficulty in, allow all the habits of the others bother me, it will create a tiny leak that will let the sea fill all the space and sink my ship.

Sometimes I need to be alone in my ship. I need to meditate, to pray and to rest. But also, I need a time to be apart from the others so to come again to them and feel the newness of their love and friendship and to be able to enter into their fun without it sinking me.

Happiness is like any other part of our lives—we must use wisdom in seeking it. We too often rush headlong into something that seems to be instant happiness, all the time telling ourselves we can right the wrong at a later time. But happiness does not remain happiness for very long when it has such strings attached.

In order to be happy we concentrate on getting, but it is giving that we find most necessary to mix into every moment. It may seem elusive, but all the things necessary are there, hidden within man himself.

Thoreau once wrote, "Time is but the stream I go fishing in."

We bait a lot of hooks in our time. We throw out a line here and a net there in hopes of finding something worthwhile to reel in. Our first impulse is to meet the tug on our line halfway and begin wading in the edge of the stream. Then, it becomes a game of wits. Can we reel in something worth carrying home? Or will it play us little by little until we are in water over our heads?

It takes an alert fisherman to go fishing in the stream of life. It takes a lot of steps when we are not sure what is beneath our feet. It wouldn't hurt us to kneel down once in a while—even in the water.

Promises are sometimes like the barber's sign, FREE HAIRCUTS TOMORROW. It is a tease that keeps someone's attention, but never quite makes good the promise.

When we are down and out in attitude, we need to be asked the question asked of Joshua, "What are you doing there on your face? Get up!"

It is more of a command than a question that jerks us upright out of our "big deep." It sets us out on our feet to do something about what has gotten us down in the first place.

We can always rise above ourselves. We are guilty of blocking our own answers and solutions because they would rob us of our self-pity. We have to be free of self-pity to be happy. And to be free we have to find something to do, something constructive to think about, something to get up off our face for, and something in which we can lovingly lose ourselves. This is rising above ourselves.

10

Increased knowledge;
increased concern . . .

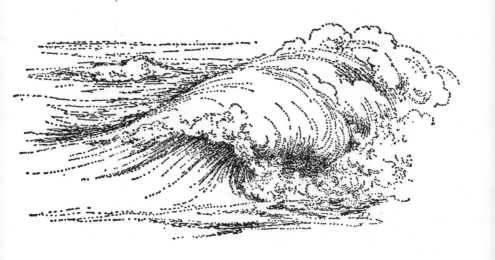

O worker of the universe! We would pray
to thee to let the irresistible current of thy
universal energy come like the impetuous south wind
of spring, let it come rushing over the vast fields
of the life of man, let it bring the scent of many
flowers, the murmurings of many woodlands, let it
make sweet and vocal the lifelessness of our dried
up soul-life. Let our newly awakened powers cry
out for unlimited fulfillment in leaf and flower
and fruit.

Rabindranath Tagore

Hardly anyone has escaped a little heavy-duty living. If we have escaped it, we should not be too proud because snobs come in all shapes and on all levels.

Neither are we to be ashamed of any struggle we may have had in our lives. It serves only to temper us to stronger foundations. Today is the only time with which we must concern ourselves. If duty or thought or circumstance weighs heavily on us, we have only to know that each moment takes difficulty farther away. Time brings happiness a tat closer every moment that we set our minds in that direction.

No regrets is a hard rule to practice. If something we have done wrong can be helped, we should make the effort. From there the plan should never include anything to regret. The main idea of not regretting is to forget the things about which we can do nothing.

Crying over all that has gone can endure for a time. After that a new cycle begins, and we have to close the old and aim for the new.

Sometimes no regrets means giving up self-pity and prejudice against optimism, but most of all it means getting on with the living.

❋

"Why should we import rags and relics into the new hour?" asked Ralph Waldo Emerson.

The mountain stream, framed in flowers and crystal clear, flows with rhythmic movement, mirroring the tall pines and cliffs that overhang from majestic heights. Aspens shimmering gold, reflect their color and pick up the color of a beverage can caught in a rock.

A wooded land, all kinds of trees—firs, elms and ashes —shading the area to a perpetual morning, surrounding a little meadow gold with flowers and strewn with old kitchen appliances no longer used.

A splendid acreage cultivated in crops, rich and lush; earth turned up by the shining plow, prepared for another season and dotted everywhere with broken-down buildings patched with rusty tin and never to be used again.

The law of connection between spiritual and material things is very precise. We can read the character of people by that which they allow to collect around them. We clutter our land, our streams and our air with every conceivable thing available, and most of the time we are not even conscious of it.

Nature works very hard to cover over the dilapidated castoffs of man. Vines hide, weather rusts and dirt covers, but it takes time and man is very quick.

Is it because we become so accustomed to where we are that we do not see the litter around us? Or do we just ignore it?

We have become so tolerant of ignorance. And the danger of it is that we become tolerant of our own. Society puts down its taproot within each of us, and if we feed that root with ignorance, what can we expect to produce? It is said that rags and tatters and dirt are always in the mind before they are on the body, so they must be in our consciousness before they can be on our land.

Only by refusing to let ourselves become ignorant can we immunize the whole of society against gross ignorance. We do not have to sacrifice the things that are dear to us, but by lifting our conscious awareness of what is good we can stop creating ugliness.

Ignorance of beauty is not a thing in passing. It is something that must be dealt with and pruned out. It is exactly like the crab grass that grows faster and is more noticeable than anything else on the front lawn. And with all that man surrounds himself and places on the front lawn, can there be any doubt about what is inside?

The will to change things for the better must be very strong. Half-hearted desires have never supplied the necessary strength to make anything work. The intention must be strong, the action determined, or else the result will be one of disappointment.

When the first wave of zeal passes, our courage wavers. It is then that we have to fortify our will to succeed. We do so by firm and quiet directions to our thoughts that we are going to accomplish what we have set out to do. Living by this rule will crumble the small obstacles and enable us to stride over the big ones.

The will to live and to live well is our decision. Coupled with faith, the will to go forward makes all things possible.

The same creative law that made a leaf built a universe.

Something very small is just as complete and beautiful in itself as something large. A little problem is just as complete and onerous as a major problem until put into perspective.

We are inclined toward getting life out of proportion, thinking the large more important than the seemingly insignificant. But the small so frequently cast such long shadows as to completely hide the greatest and most important.

How can we judge the great and the small? By having a sense of true perspective within ourselves for ourselves and then for all other creation.

How can we believe it possible to mold our lives the way we want them? There are probably ten good reasons why that is not possible. But there are a dozen more why it is definitely possible.

Our greatest uncertainty is because we have no main plan. If we were suddenly given the traditional three wishes, we would be too stunned, too disorderly, too incomplete to know exactly what we would ask for or even want to receive.

To have a dream is necessary. To have a design for life is necessary. We must have faith in it. We must be willing to be criticized for it and take actual steps toward it.

Knowledge, study and measuring are basic. Doing is the ultimate necessity.

11

*Wisdom
excells shallowness;
light transcends darkness . . .*

~~~~~~

*Love is the river of life in this world.
Think not that ye know it who stand at the little
tinkling rill, the first small fountain.*

*Not until you have gone through the rocky
gorges, and not lost the stream; not until you have
gone through the meadow, and the stream has
widened and deepened until fleets could ride on its
bosom; not until beyond the meadow you have
come to the unfathomable ocean, and poured your
treasures into its depths—not until then can you
know what love is.*

Henry Ward Beecher

Talleyrand wrote, "If you wish to appear agreeable in society, you must consent to be taught many things which you know already."

Is there some inner-knowing that is not weighed down with recorded facts? Man is not programed to instinct as is nature, but he recognizes a truth when he hears it so that truth must already be within him.

It seems that anything we really know is there and just has to be called into consciousness before we can claim it as our own.

Patience shows intelligence, it is said. We keep wanting to do something, move ahead and do and plan and insist on things happening. But E. Stanley Jones said, "The streams that turn the machinery of the world take their rise in silent places."

Power comes from the deep silence we sometimes must experience before we can gain enough momentum to move ahead in our living. Patience is never dormant, but a very definite action that provides the blueprint for action, dimension, direction and fortitude to go farther than we ever dreamed possible.

The earth is moving, but we cannot see it. Patience

is doing its perfect work, and we cannot see that either. But we will when we see the changes taking place in our own natures.

A great teacher once taught, "If any man wants to be first, then he shall be last of all and servant of all."

We seldom realize what it means to be first in the eyes of man. It means last in line and in the service of all.

Man does not have to be humble to be in first place, but he has to be humble to stay there. In a sense, he has to open every door and wait until everyone has gone through before he enters. Then he personally serves others or waits to the last to be served.

The man who wants to be first must learn the lesson and gain the wisdom of being willing to be last.

It felt good to have the sun warm on my head as I strung white sheets along the clothesline to dry. The air was so fresh and clean after the succession of storms, and the linens would come in smelling sweet and flower fresh.

Even the calm quiet was a welcome experience after having had so many warnings because of the summer storms. And even while I was thinking of the warnings the sound of sirens split the air with long, whining, ugly sounds. Stunned by the sound coming out of a perfectly clear, blue sky, I stood motionless wondering what had happened to cause the sirens to blow. Before I could move I heard running footsteps, and a neighbor lady from down the block burst through the garden gate followed by her five offspring. They said nothing but ran straight toward the cellar which stood open for airing. They had just disappeared underground when it dawned on me how panicky they were.

I went inside to the telephone and called the city offices, "What are the sirens blowing for this time?"

"Nothing, lady," a gruff voice answered, evidently having been asked that already a number of times. "We just have a little short in the electronic equipment and we are repairing it now."

I sat down to enjoy a cup of coffee after I had convinced my frightened neighbors that it was all a mistake, and it dawned on me how little faith we have in our own common sense.

We tend to wait in groups to be herded in this way and that, even when we know it is wrong. We panic instead of looking up and seeing that there is not a cloud in the sky. We, as a people, are conditioned and organized to stampede toward things that are not to our benefit.

We cannot ignore our wisdom in heeding warnings and avoiding difficulty, but we have the ability to think, and we should have more faith in our own competence.

At times we have high hopes instead of faith. We always hope something we want very much is in the offing. How much real faith do we have that it is?

The whole thing hinges on where we place our faith. Too many times it is based on the tangible things we expect to come through to help us. Some of it is based on what others can do for us, the connections we have. And then we go to the strength of our backs and hope our capabilities are greater than we realize.

We do have to believe in ourselves. We have to believe in other people, but true faith is something we have to practice in the face of all that says it is not real. It is a gift that we receive joyfully and maintain constantly with a positive attitude. It is a "knowing" that we are never alone.

Learning is the only advancing flame that cannot be extinguished.

Whatever we choose to think and do and be, when we find we have unlimited span within our minds to move and be free, then there is absolutely nothing that can hold us back.

We are the ones who put stops in our minds to shut off advancement. When we think we cannot learn anything new it becomes almost impossible for anyone to teach us.

When we are willing to learn, no matter what the age, we are teachable, and whatever knowledge we gain is ours. No one can take it from us.

The desire to know is a flame that cannot be extinguished. This is education.

12

*There is
nothing new
under the sun . . .*

Truth is always in us. There is nothing new under the sun. All we have to do is learn how to handle what we already are. . . .

Ruth Given Jacques

"This time, like all other times, is a very good one, if we but know what to do with it."

Emerson's words are as true today as they were in his time. The chaos of the hour is not something new but only appears in a different form. When we begin to live in fear and dread of the future we must remember that progress is always upward. We, individually, slow it or help it, and we do it by correcting what can be corrected within our own jurisdiction and by boosting and encouraging what is right. Each of us controls the swing of the pendulum.

Events of the day are not new, but our approach to them must take a fresh turn.

Equality? Yes, I believe in it! I believe in the equality of the individual, which has nothing at all to do with race, creed, color or sex. No one has the world cornered on superiority, but each person has the right to rise to whatever heights he is able to envision. It all has to do with what we have our eye fastened on.

Oh, there's nothing new about the battle of the sexes . . . that one started with the beginning of time.

Emerson said that all things are double, one against the other . . . measure for measure—love for love—give and take. Seems to me it's forty-sixty anyway you look at it. First forty-sixty this way and then forty-sixty that way, but seldom, if ever, fifty-fifty. Human beings are not that well co-ordinated, nor do they keep score so precisely . . . not if they really care, that is.

Intelligence is not always on the side of the dominant, nor is weakness always on the side of those who are dominated. It is what we, as individuals, want to be, and it is what we want those around us to be.

The woman is the symbol of the soul and man the sign of strength. And yet, great strength is required to bear a child, and some of our most understanding and gentle men have been leaders in history.

There is a polarity in every part of nature. There are wrongs done, but there are also compensations. The more equality we have the more responsibility we have, and that responsibility is not always where we can see it. We are all like cups of water—when we are poured into a great container we are a part of the great whole and cannot be divided out as we were before.

There are those who want to compete, and there are others who have no desire and no need for competition.

It is not always the one who cries the loudest that is the most deeply hurt. There is even competition within every individual—one desire against another. Some women are so domineering that if they asked for more privileges they would have to go the other way . . . and some men in their efforts to control stand close to being dictators, and dictators go down the drain every day.

Somehow it seems safer for both to be willing to let the other have a part in the game. It is according to what we want in life and how we go about getting it. Some feel superior by demanding and getting while others prefer the honey method . . . it all goes back to the individual.

Emerson says every man is a god playing a fool. Perhaps we are not aware of this . . . and thus, we keep asking for something we already have. There's nothing new under the sun.

Certain knowledgeable sources tell us that our body cells renew and regenerate themselves on a continual basis. Then why do we ever grow old? Could it be our thought is the same "old" thought?

As children, have we not all scurried along some hidden path like rabbits, or thrilled to special hideaways that we were sure no one else knew existed?

Something within us never really grows up. We still cherish a moment of solitude away from the beaten path. The feeling may come in a crowd where everyone is a stranger unquestioning, requiring nothing of us. It may be a walk in the woods where nature's wildlife becomes very quiet or ignores us completely. Or it may be behind closed doors where noise is shut out and peace reigns within.

Wherever or whatever we require to make us feel the comfort of solitude, it is first begun in the heart and thoughts in a feeling of contentment, a willingness and an ability to enjoy a retreat like that of childhood.

Thank You for the rain drops, for the cool evening breezes, for the rose-streaked sky after the shower. Thank You for the locust's song, for sounds of sleepy birds, for the companionship of my dog as we walk in silence through the twilight. Nothing new. The old is ever young and beautiful and excellent.

Of all the old things under the sun, love must ever be the newest. The happy and fulfilled acclaim it wonderful. The bitter and cynical have other things to say. And Henry David Thoreau had this to relate, ". . . if he is weak in the knees let him not call the hill steep."

We tend to blame all that we do not have on circumstances and other people when the answer is really that we must be loving and capable of being loved.

Whole lifetimes are wasted because "the principle of the thing" was not in keeping. Our inability to forgive and to give has kept us from being good partners, good parents, good friends.

We should not let our weak knees keep us from what is rightfully and happily ours because we could not let our bitterness go.

Nothing so makes the old become all new—like love.

150.13

HIFLER

2145

All rivers run to the sea.

**PLEASE RETURN
IN TWO WEEKS**